101 Uses for a Dead Computer

Compiled by Mat Wahlstrom and Illustrated by Ted Pitts

101 Uses for a Dead Computer

Library of Congress Catalog No.: 92-74276

ISBN: 0-672-48540-0

94   93   92   4   3   2   1

Interpretation of the printing code: the rightmost double-digit number is the year of the book's printing; the rightmost single-digit number is the number of the book's printing. For example, a printing code of 92-1 shows that the first printing of the book occurred in 1992.

About the Compiler — Mat Wahlstrom

A devout Sagittarian possessed with many peripheral and often obscure devotions, Mat likes very few things to the exclusion of others and believes a good deal. A devastatedly handsome poet, he is also the fanciful author of *Anybody's Mat Book*, *The Dead Mat Scrolls*, Hayden's *Cool Mat* series, and *Nude Computing for Windows: Tips, Tricks, and Traps*.

About the Illustrator — Ted Pitts

A free-lance illustrator who, aside from some down-time for law school and a stint as a newspaper artist, has been drawing dragons and spaceships since he was four. He lives in Xenia, Ohio with the lovely Susan — his wife, and the almost-perfect Andy — his son. He owns an SE-30 and wants a Harley.

We Want to Hear from You

What our readers think of Hayden is crucial to our sense of well-being. If you have any comments, no matter how great or how small, we'd appreciate your taking the time to send us a note, fax us a fax, rhyme us a rhyme, etc.

Mike Britton, Publisher
Hayden
11711 N. College Ave. (a boring address, but we assure you we're anything but boring)
Carmel, IN (yes, Indiana—not California...) 46032
(317) 573-6880 voice, (317) 571-3484 fax,
AppleLink: HAYDEN.BOOKS, America Online: MikeHayden, CompuServe: 76350,3014

If this book has changed your life, please write and describe the euphoria you've experienced. If you have a cool idea of your own creation, please send it (caged, of course) directly to us at Hayden. Who knows? Your creation may end up in *101 Uses for a Dead Computer: The Sequel.*

Acknowledgments

This book began as one of many topics in an after-lunch discussion between Patrick Ames and the Hayden staff. The service was prompt, the furnishings posh, and the bill most pricey, so I guess it's good that we have something to show for the expense report. After a couple of passably funny memos to everyone at Prentice Hall Computer Publishing, we got enough ideas to start thinking of whom to get to actually write the book. As I wrote these passably funny memos, Mike Britton decided that I could write a passably funny book. And while I may have proved him wrong, I'm grateful for the opportunity no matter what. The list of the wonderful and imaginative PHCP employees et al. who contributed ideas is presented seperately, so let me here thank the "non-authoring" personnel who were absolutely indispensible in bringing about this book: Jay Corpus, M. T. Cagnina, and Mike Miller. Finally, I would like to express my gratitude to whomever the heck it was who discovered caffeine. Enjoy!

Trademark Acknowledgments

Contributors

Rebecca Arnoff, Scott Boucher, Paula Carroll, Lori Cates, Curt Cox, Stephen Dierckes, Jerry Dunn, Tony Eijkelenboom, Jennifer Flynn, Tim Groeling, Steve Haigh, Stacy Hiquet, Eric Hoffman, Lisa Hoffman, Phil Kitchel, Richard Leach, Beth Ann Lucas, Karen Opal, San Dee Phillips, Ted Pitts, David Remington, Susan Shaw, Sandra Shay, Kevin Spear, Ann Taylor, Martha Thieme, Hugh Vandivier, Lisa Wagner, Faithe Wempen, Robert Waring, and my redoubtable fellow Haydenizens—Mike Britton, Dave Ciskowski, Marj Hopper, Karen Whitehouse, and Laura Wirthlin.

1 Garage Sale

Why do people go to garage sales except to buy awful stuff that they know they'll never use? Put out your old computer and dot matrix printer and tell them it's one of those funky printout-banner-makers that are so nifty for those office birthday and pink-slip parties.

2 Hood Ornament

From the freaky Futurist clover of the Mercedes logo to the chromium nymph on the Rolls-Royce grill, the hood ornament commands instant recognition and trumpets an owner's status to legions of subcompact drivers and hip-hop fashion victims everywhere. But how can you express yourself to a fleeting world as someone other than a mere luxury sedan enthusiast or MTV zombie? Mount a Mac Classic

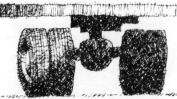

on the front of your Mack truck! (Or a PC on your Peterbilt—the point is to try to buck those stereotypes.) Here's an unforgettable way to say "I may be blue collar, but I'm System 7-savvy."

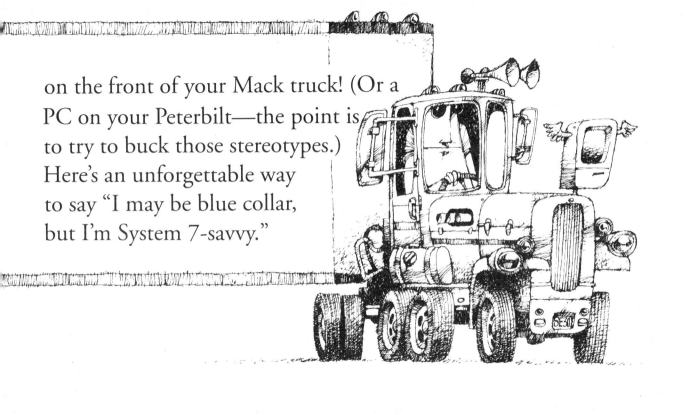

3   Party PC

Create your own party favor that will be a party favorite: have your old computer handy for guests to record their anecdotes, deep thoughts, and drunken reveries. Amuse your friends and amaze the alcoholics long afterwards when you capture the moment on hard disk!

4 Mousemat

Cushy, folksy, and colorful, nothing welcomes more than a home-made mousepad doormat. So functional yet decorative, you'll have to take it in at night to keep the neighbors from swiping it!

5 Elvis Database

Oh, sure: *other* people always see Elvis at the super mini-mart or lube shop, but *you* always find out too late. Create an Elvis-sighting database to correlate all the geographic points and lunar phases, and figure out *in time* where The King will be next!

6 Jewelry

A high-tech high-fashion statement.

7 Bingo

Need a sure-fire way to eliminate the worry of which Lotto combinations to pick or how to "call out" the numbers during those rousing bouts of solitaire bingo? Just program your old computer to be a fixed-parameter random number generator, and the probabilities are endless.

8   Clock Alarm

Do you hate mornings? Do you spend more than 10% of your net income buying replacement alarm clocks for the ones you've hurled against the wall? Load up your old Mac with all the sound-capable alarm and alert-type programs you can get your hands on and be late to work no more!

9   Snack Bowl

What better way to serve your guests and take care of those 3 A.M. Prodigy-odyssey cravings for munchies than with a gutted CPU shell snack bowl? It'll be "thanks for the memory" and chips galore when you wow 'em with this little wonder.

10 Diving Helmet

Sure, it's no longer a big deal for you to see fish on computer screens anymore—but just think how it will freak out those real little fishies to see *you* on a computer screen! Simply empty and waterseal and you can bring all the joys of DOS to the briny deep.

11 Kiosk

An electronic bulletin board even Grandma can access.

12 Bean Count Contest Holder

Guess the right amount and win a date with the richest man in the Word!

13 Piñata

Bid a final ¡Olé! to OLE!

14 Puppet Show Stage

Encourage your own future Jim Hensons and Edgar Bergens by taking out all the sharp nasties and giving them the terminal shell as their very own finger theater! You'll enjoy listening to the endless hours of fun they'll have practicing to be little Geraldos and Sally Jesses, too...

15 Time Capsule Artifact

If you think *you* had problems with Turbo Pascal, just think of the difficulties your great-great-great-grandchildren will have figuring out what possible *use* something like that could have (once they get that Kaypro working again). "Stump eternity" is the name of this game!

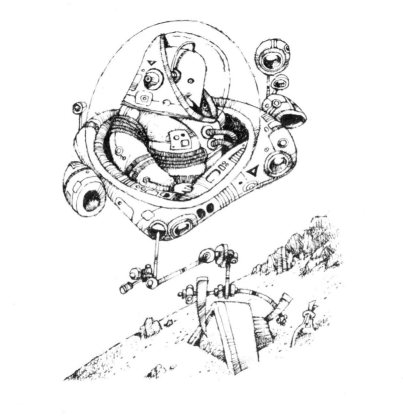

16 Charitable Donation

Clearly a good deal of what constitutes an old or worthless computer is perception. For many worthwhile non-profit organizations and needy individuals, your computer is just the thing for their administrative, database storage, or Super Bowl bet pool needs. And don't forget to claim the deduction on your taxes!

17 Flagpole Finial

Every patriotic hacker should have one.

18 Lawn Ornament

A GUI garden gnome!

19 Canoe Paddle

Have a toggle that boggles by making some handy-dandy keyboard paddles. Whether you're planning on shooting the whitewater in a kayak or a performance art interpretation of the "Song of Hiawatha," make sure you use the paddle that gives you Ctrl.

20 Drafting Program Support

Give your PC a prosthesis and your fingers a break by connecting your old computer terminal to your newer computer to run the text screen while you run the graphics on the other. Yes, you guessed it—turn your old computer into an AutoCADdy!

21 Test Case

Want to upgrade your computer but don't want to risk its ruination? Dust off your neighbor's old computer and practice installing extra RAM in it instead. Experiment with different components, mix and match, and maybe, just maybe, you could have that TRS-80 performing like a Cray.

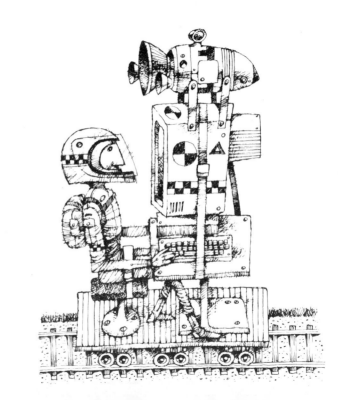

22 Viral Protection

In a world where Michaelangelo is no longer the name of a towering artist, but the moniker of electric viruses and hard-shelled reptiles, the only thing truly sacred is a good idea (or one that sells—it's tough to tell). Refit and reformat your old computer to run only one (or many, depending on how paranoid you are) of the available virus detection software packages. You need never worry about your *real* computer again. What's the old saying about women and children first?

23 Bungee Cord Tester

Your personal bungee cord tester.

24 Recipe Holder

Introduce your Mom to the power of personal computing: empty that midget Mac hard drive of all files and load up a HyperCard stack for her recipes. No longer will she have to hunt and scatter looking for that tattered zucchini bread blueprint from 1954, and before long she'll start to get that crazed look in her eyes whenever "extra RAM" is mentioned.

25 Knobs

Got a worthless printer with a platen? Then that cabinet-refinishing job is as good as done when you use its old knobs as door pulls. (Extra neat if you use the cabinet to store your floppies!)

26 Traffic Cones

Just paint those old PCs fluorescent orange for traffic cones that *no* joyrider will want to run over. If only network traffic could be fixed so easily...

27 Pool Table Accessory

And you'll never wait in a "cue" line again.

28 Carrying Case

Tired of having your alligator leather, eel skin, ostrich hide, and forest-friend flesh valises beaten to pieces? Do you desire a strong yet light, ultra chic briefcase—one that can go from the CEO power brunch to the ASPCA meeting and not miss a fashion beat? Then gut that imaginatively rectangular drive casing, break out your handy-dandy pocket spot welder, and you've got yourself the executive accessory of the '90s. Artfully replace sections of the circuit boards to make dividers for portable fax and Mont Blanc pen compartments. Who needs the Sharper Image when you can have the Soho/Tokyo "look"?

29 Memo Alert

Tired of hearing your kids complain about hearing you remind them to take care of those household chores? Program your computer to do the nagging for you. The endless requests it takes to get the tykes to fly to their tasks need never irritate you again!

30 Outdoor Footlights

Upgrade your garden path and take a walk down "memory" lane...

31 Scarecrow Heads

Is this what some people mean by DOS for dummies?

32 Coffee Table

With a glass top from Pier 1 Imports and the right animation or screen protection program, you too can have the ultimate coffee table. It'll be just perfect in providing that low-intensity, indirect lighting so essential for intimate conversations and Avon visits.

33 Terrarium

A terrific terminal terrarium.

34 Used Store

Take your old computer and everyone else's you can find (if they haven't seen this book) and start a used computer store. Make even more money by renting it/them to students who invariably pull the all-nighters which keep them from using the better campus models for free!

35 Exercise Bike Mount

Programmed landscapes created while-you-sweat.

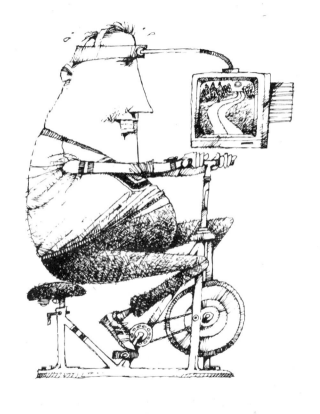

36 Targets

Do you need urban preparedness training? Or is junior earning a Musketry merit badge and you don't want to "shell" out the bucks for a target range membership? Just set up your old computer and soon you'll be singing "Takin' It to the Skeets."

37 Home Budget Center

All it takes is the right spreadsheet program and a little tinkering to have a home budget center that the whole family can use to actually see just how darn expensive things are nowadays.

38 Dance Floor

Since disco is dead, why not a dead computer disco floor?

39 Book Ends

Although you may need to wait until your next computer is finally a dead computer, the delay will be worth the wait when you spice up that library shelf or den nook with a (matching?) set of computer bookends. As a special treat, use them to prop up your archaeology, ancient history, and *Using Lisa* books.

40 Mod Clothing

Clothes that speak a declarative language.

41 Music Show Decor

Lend your old computer to your favorite thrash metal-heads as a stage prop, and give them creative license to do with it what they will. A great way to have all those components broken down for you to recycle—and to show the younger generation that you dig where their head is at.

42 BBS

Have you ever had delusions of grandeur so great that nothing less than total cosmic dominion would have meaning? Then turn your old computer into a bulletin board service or bitnet relay and make yourself Supreme SYSOP—even the Roman emperors never had such power.

43 Macramé

For limitless artsy-craftsies, color me macro-mé!

44 Weights

Get the Silicon Beach body you've always dreamed of !

45 Trophy

Do you know a hacker who needs more hardware like he needs a hole in his head-seek-time? Spray paint your old computer gold, attach a plaque, and give it to him as an "online achievement award." He might just look away from his screen long enough to cry...

46 Slaw Shredder

With just a little modification, your disk drive can make mounds of julienne fries in seconds! (After all, you remember what it could do to your disks, don't you?)

47 Therapy Tool

Get in touch with your rage, the hairy man within, and symbolically free yourself from the stifling conventions and rules of the workplace! Scrawl obscenities over the casing, pull the keys one-by-one from the console, and repeatedly load 4.5M programs on it in order to watch it crash. TIP: use it as a voodoo "doll" for the torment of your work computer—especially before you have to go in some sunny Friday.

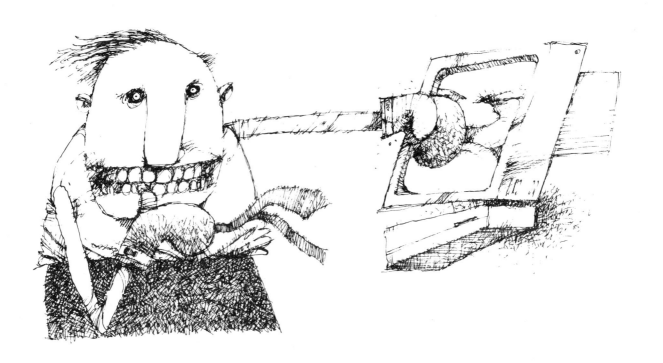

48 Skateboard

Attach the wheel trucks from a less snazzy model to the bottom of an old keyboard and you've got the ultimate cyberpunk skateboard. It will massage your feet as they do what it is you do, and give new meaning to the term "rad to the Macs!"

49 ChiAmiga

Want to make your own definitive statement on "green technology?" Need to find a way to always have those vital alfalfa sprouts around when you need them? No problem! Take an awl or similarly sharp object and grout/dig/gouge/score/mark/scratch/stab lots of little rows all over the surface of your designated computer. Get your seeds of choice, spread them with an agar jelly or some such, water and sun, and in just weeks you'll have a lush and decidedly prominent indoor garden.

50 Miniature Golf

As weird windmills and silly obstacle paths, dead computers once again make putting a hoot.

51 Bicycle Accessory

Give a mondo mod twist to the old playing-card-in-the-spokes clicker trick.

52 Planter

Want a different way to show off those hens and chicks and rose moss? Punch out different-sized holes all over your computer, fill with dirt, and your pansies will wilt in envy of their cousins' new home.

53 Ant Farm

Nature's own little database.

54 For the "Just Married"

Simply attach your dead computer to the bumper of the newlyweds' coach and let everyone know that "it's a match made in Motorola."

55 Objet d'Arts

Do you know what art is and what you don't like? Combine the two by getting as much old hardware as you can and more-or-less imaginatively welding it together. You can make boku grant money from works with names like "Mainframe IV," "Silicon Rex Imperative," "Terminal Decay," and "A Night on Baud Mountain: The Postmodemist Experience."

56 Cop Stopper

Speeding citations got you down? Just put your powerful-looking old computer in the front seat next to you with one of those lighter-adapter cords, and tell the officer that your pal HAL wasn't paying attention. Makes a great armrest, too!

57 Aquarium

Pyro! and the After Dark/More After Dark programs have revolutionized the way Mac and PC users think about terminal burnout, both as a physical defect and as a creeping personal dread. Having clearly evolved into something way, way more involving of RAM and thought than should be sanely reasonable, screen saver programs have become an end unto themselves. So what better way to both poke fun at this phenomenon and have fun at its expense than to actually *have* fish swimming inside your terminal? Just don't include any flying appliances...

58 Anchor

An anchor fit for a Commodore, or vice-versa.

59 Playground Structures

Just don't let them play "King of the Mainframe."

60 Security Alarm

Even the earliest Macs were audio-capable, so why not load up some sound files and have your old computer be your electric home sentinel? It won't shed, and no Doberman can duplicate that just-right dialogue from old "Dragnet" episodes.

61 Free T-Shirt

Want one of those nifty *Late Night with David Letterman* t-shirts but don't have a stupid pet to trick? Suggest ol' dapper Dave work one of those hydraulic press/fire tower/Velcro stunts on your defunct computer, and your newest wardrobe addition is as good as on its way.

62 Bird House

You always knew it was for the birds anyway.

63 Rear-View Mirror

Does your car's rear-view mirror cry out for some decorative expression of individuality? Far better than fuzzy dice is some quirky circuitry or worthless peripheral, and, unlike New Age crystals, you know that these actually can work.

64 Cat Toy

Looking for the perfect cat toy—one that isn't the same old, predictably ugly-colored rubber nonesuch that you wouldn't give to a dog to play with? Easy! Just detach that mouse from your keyboard, hollow it out, and fill it with catnip. You'll have as much fun as your feline when you watch the endless hours of sense-reference tumbling that will occur, and maybe learn a little about yourself and your relation to the mind-drugging toys of our time. Or maybe not.

65 Cable Helpers

Never can find a pen or lighter or remote control when you need it? Just use those old peripheral and keyboard connector cables to attach them to the ceiling—and convenience is only a recoil away!

66 Giant Game Pieces

Lisa in Wonderland.

67 Word-Game Pieces

Have you missed playing Scrabble because your slobbering baby nephew teethed his cuspids on J_8 and two E_1s in 1983 and you didn't want to fork out the bucks for a new set? Just rip those easy-to-manipulate keys from the console and you'll have a whole new alphabet of identically-shaped tiles from which to choose (if you haven't already forgotten their point values).

68 Nightlight

"Screenlight, screen bright, first screen I see tonight..."

69 Halloween

With just a little imagination and some old parts from your PC, you can have an imaginative and ready-made costume for Halloween frolics. Go by yourself as a cyborg, or get a group and be a network!

70 Jack-o'-Lantern

Eek! A Mac-o'-Lantern!

71 Doll House

Generally, the older the computer is, the bigger it gets, and all that bulk and space that was once filled with circuitry can now be filled with your children's imagination. Endless hours of peace and quiet are yours when your old dedicated Digital becomes a mini beach condo or guerrilla training camp for your little ones and their figurative figurines.

72 Science Project

Are you sick of hearing your kids beg for a TV of their very own in their room, but don't want to have to shell out the bucks for a new Sony? Just turn them loose in a Heathkit store and have them turn that terminal into their very own "crystal TV" set. Who knows, maybe they'll pick up Channel 3, Argentina?

(Alas, even dead computer humor can die. Heathkit recently got out of the kit business.)

73 Letter Box

Looking for a heavy-duty way to protect your catalog-ordered software before you're able to get it inside? With just a few alterations, that old computer can become the most talked-about mailbox in the tri-county area, and everything at your end will be "PC, Mr. Postman."

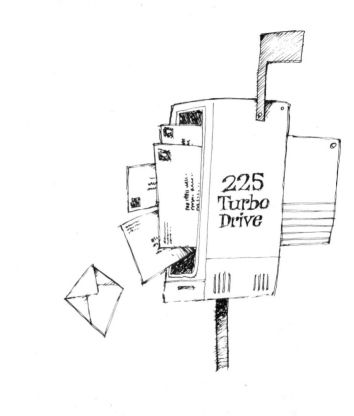

74 Tax Shelter

It seems a shame to fork out all that money on hardware, software, upgrades, die-cut neon mousepads, and not be able to get some of the loot back. So claim your system as a dependent to the IRS! After all, if it wasn't beloved family, would you be spending that much on it?

75 Fridge Magnets

User-friendly magnetic media.

76 Cornucopia

Hollow out your dead computer and fill it with all of nature's bounty for a horn of plenty that's ripe with the nostalgia of Silicon Valley Thanksgivings of yore.

77 Breakfast Tray

Wondering how to treat your mate after he forgot your anniversary? Give him breakfast in bed and use that old Mac Portable as the breakfast tray! Sure it will probably cut off the circulation in his lower body, but you'll enjoy how he tries to ignore this rather than risk upsetting you again.

78 Kiddie Office Accessory

In the future, everyone will use computers; and the future is today. You don't have to be Yuppie scum to want, or be able, to have your kid comfortable and financially functional in the global marketplace. After playing with just a few simple data entry programs, you'll blink twice in order to recognize the difference between the kids and your co-workers.

79 Arcade

Use your old computer as the starting point for setting up your own computer games arcade. Scour garage sales and flea markets for joysticks, other old computers, and sundry peripherals, and watch your little venture take off! (Be sure to set up a file server/share monitor for yourself to cut off those who try to go over their time limit.)

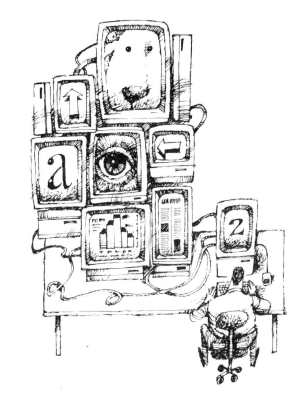

80 Back-Up Device

Worried about file flight and system suicide, but don't want to take up hard drive space and speed to protect yourself? Set up your old computer's hard drive so that it's the destination of all your (automatic) file back-ups. The presence of mind that can only come from safe computing will be yours again.

81 Self-Help Typing

Yes, it *is* a radical idea, but imagine loading a typewriting program on your old computer to actually learn to become more than a hunt-and-peck hacker. And for aspiring secretaries, it's a must!

82 Salt & Pepper Shakers

Pass the peripherals, please...

83 Aerial Bombs

Yet another way for a computer to bomb.

84 Rolodex

With some simple coding and an old modem, you, too, can have an automatic-dial "ROModex" to find and make all your phone calls. Again, with all the technology available, why *shouldn't* you needlessly complicate even the most trivial of day-to-day operations?

85 Tiles

Double-density in a dozen colors!

86 Crash Helmet

Show the gang at work what a *real* "illegal character" looks like.

87 Vanity Mirror

Do you know one of those people who have never seen anything in computers to interest them? Try tricking them by giving them an old computer with a silvered, completely reflecting screen. (Or, leave an unexposed ribbon around the screen's edge for that make-up mirror effect). In no time at all you'll be hearing "PC, PC, on the dresser; who's fairer than an Intel processor?

88 Magazine Rack

Where, oh, where to keep those back issues of *ComputerWorld* and *MacWeek* but in an upright and emptied CP unit shell? You won't know whether it's the back issues or clever design concept that keep your guests in the bathroom so long!

89 Piggy Bank

When it's full, you *might* be able to buy another.

90 Doorstop

Guaranteed to keep any door open (even in hurricane-force gales). This doorstop is also a good idea when you want to make sure your 16-year-old daughter is okay when her boyfriend, the school's leather rebel, comes over to "study" in her room.

91 Vocabulary Builder

Do you have the Oxford English Dictionary on CD-ROM, but find the book format so much easier? Plug the CD player into your old computer, set it on random select, and you need never sedulously cogitate upon actuating a thesaurus afresh.

92 Prop

See how much of a premium you can make by selling your dead computer to a furniture store, photo studio, civic theater, or office wanting to *look* automated—the perfect prop for perpetrating their particular pretense. Pretty puckish, no?

93 Trash Bin

Why deny yourself the thrill of trashing files just because your icons don't drag like they used to? Simply cut and gut and you'll have your own modern equivalent of the elephant leg can of yesteryear.

94 Propaganda

Single-handedly bring the former Eastern Bloc countries up from the 1950s to the 1980s with your old computer donation(s). Now you can meet the needs of that hungry protocapitalist marketplace with the wonders of QWERTY and CP/M.

95 Game Balls

Imagine the irony of playing marbles with cat's eyes and mouse bearings, or bocci with turbo tracking balls—or have I subreferenced just once too often?

96 Andirons

When winter winds make you weak
  and your hearth a style it lacks—a
just snuggle up in front of a roaring file
  and be glad you don't live in Alaska.

97 An Ahistorical Moment

Statesman, General, Father of His Country, Mac Fanatic.

98 Gift

Don't know what to get that anonymous acquaintance for whom you have to get a combination gift, consolation, Christmas, and door prize? Look no further than your old computer. Just imagine the cost they'll go to to try and top you when it's your turn to receive!

99 Holiday Display

Dreaming of a white noise Xmas.

100 Snowshoes

Invert and convert two useless old keyboards with rivets and straps and you've got the perfect flexible-tread snowshoes for the white and wild. They leave incredible tracks, and the tales of "Nanook of the NETNORTH" will inspire for generations.

101 Recycle

After all, there's nothing funny about pollution.